Paul's Perilous Journey

Paul's Perilous Journey

by
John MacArthur, Jr.

WORD OF GRACE COMMUNICATIONS
P.O. Box 4000
Panorama City, CA 91412

Library of Congress Cataloging in Publication Data

MacArthur, John, 1939-
    Paul's perilous journey / by John MacArthur, Jr.
       p.   cm. — (John MacArthur's Bible studies)
    Includes indexes.
    ISBN 0-8024-5350-3
    1. Bible.   N.T.   Acts XVII, 1-26—Criticism, interpretation, etc.
  2. Paul, the Apostle, Saint—Journeys—Mediterranean Region.
  I. Title.   II. Series: MacArthur, John, 1939-   Bible studies.
  BS2625.2.M273   1989
  226'.6077—dc19   89-3393
                                         CIP

1 2 3 4 5 Printing/LC/Year 92 91 90 89

Printed in the United States of America

Contents

These Bible studies are taken from messages delivered by Pastor-Teacher John MacArthur, Jr., at Grace Community Church in Panorama City, California. These messages have been combined into a 4-tape album entitled *Paul's Perilous Journey*. You may purchase this series either in an attractive vinyl cassette album or as individual cassettes. To purchase these tapes, request the album *Paul's Perilous Journey*, or ask for the tapes by their individual GC numbers. Please consult the current price list; then, send your order, making your check payable to:

WORD OF GRACE COMMUNICATIONS
P.O. Box 4000
Panorama City, CA 91412

Or call the following toll-free number:
1-800-55-GRACE

1
Paul's Journey to Rome—Part 1

Outline

Introduction
A. The Practice of Seamanship
B. The Providence of God
C. The Personality of Paul
   1. His labor
   2. His leadership

Lesson
I. The Passage
  A. The Start (vv. 1-8)
    1. The participants (v. 1*a*, 2*b*)
     a) Paul's traveling companions
     b) Festus's allowance
    2. The prisoners (v. 1*c*)
     a) The duties of centurions
     b) The integrity of centurions
    3. The port (v. 2*a*)
    4. The permission (v. 3)
     a) The church at Sidon
     b) The refreshment of Paul
    5. The problems (v. 4)
     a) The winds
     b) The weather
    6. The pilgrimage (vv. 5-6)
     a) The ship's origin (v. 5)
     b) The centurion's opportunity (v. 6)
    7. The slow progress (vv. 7-8)
     a) The danger (v. 7)
     b) The difficulty (v. 8)

B. The Stay (vv. 9-12)
   1. Paul's concern about the voyage (vv. 9-10)
      a) The weather (v. 9a)
      b) The timing (v. 9b)
      c) The warning (vv. 9c-10)
   2. The centurion's choice to go on (vv. 11-12)
      a) The men in charge (v. 11)
      b) The majority who chose (v. 12)
C. The Storm (vv. 13-26)
   1. The deceptive breezes (v. 13)
   2. The destructive tempest (v. 14)
   3. The driven ship (vv. 15-17)
      a) Looking for protection (vv. 15-16a)
      b) Preparing the ship (vv. 16b-17)
         (1) They secured the lifeboat (v. 16b)
         (2) They undergirded the ship (v. 17a)
         (3) They struck the sail (v. 17b)
   4. The desperate measures (vv. 18-20)
      a) Lightening the load (v. 18)
      b) Casting the tackle (v. 19)
      c) Abandoning hope (v. 20)
   5. The divine comfort (vv. 21-26)
      a) The lack of food (v. 21)
      b) The failure to listen (v. 21b)
      c) The preservation of life (v. 22)
      d) The trustworthiness of God (vv. 23-26)

Introduction

A. The Practice of Seamanship

Acts 27 describes one of three shipwrecks that the apostle Paul endured (2 Cor. 11:25). This chapter is one of the most detailed in all Scripture. Historians and archaeologists have studied this passage for its valuable description of ancient seamanship. There's much to learn about how people conducted their work on the seas, particularly in times of crisis.

B. The Providence of God

Throughout the passage it is clear who was really in control of the events and elements. As easily as Jesus Christ could calm the wind and waves (Matt. 8:23-27), so God could stir them up for His own ends. And when it pleased Him to calm the seas to make Himself known, He did.

C. The Personality of Paul

Paul, the dominant personality in the drama of Acts 27, experienced many trials in his life, and this journey was no different. The true mettle of a person shines forth in the fires of testing. Crises reveal character.

1. His labor

This particular journey was perhaps the most prolonged, intense, and unrelenting crisis Paul ever endured. He started off already fatigued by imprisonment and then faced wind and waves, sword-bearing soldiers, and finally poisonous snakes. He was imperiled in his journey from beginning to end.

2. His leadership

Nevertheless, throughout the journey Paul was calm, courageous, and confident. He was always a true leader. He started the trip as a prisoner, yet ended up commanding everyone, including the captain, the sailing master, and the Roman centurion. The characteristics of true spiritual leadership are all exemplified in the life of the apostle Paul.

Lesson

I. THE PASSAGE

A. The Start (vv. 1-8)

Ever since the Holy Spirit planted in Paul's mind the idea of going to Rome, he never lost confidence in the fulfillment of that plan. He had been to Jerusalem to deliver contributions to the poor saints there (Acts 21:15; 1 Cor. 16:3), and now he earnestly desired to go to Rome. However, the angry Jewish population had kept him imprisoned for two years. At the end of that time he appealed to Caesar, and his case was transferred to Rome.

1. The participants (v. 1*a*, 2*b*)

"When it was determined that we should sail . . . Aristarchus, a Macedonian of Thessalonica, being with us."

The use of "we" in verse 1 and "us" in verse 2 is a return to the "we" of Acts 21:18, an indication that Luke—the writer of the book of Acts—had since rejoined Paul. Luke had most likely been living in Caesarea, where Paul was imprisoned, and had joined him along with Aristarchus, a Macedonian from Thessalonica.

a) Paul's traveling companions

Paul's trip to Rome was made in the company of two of his dearest friends, which is remarkable considering it was unheard of for a prisoner to be allowed companions. There were two ways this allowance could have taken place: they would either have had to take the position as slaves of Paul or get special permission from Festus, the governor before whom Paul appealed to Rome.

b) Festus's allowance

Festus, knowing the innocence of Paul, might have wanted to secure his good reputation with Rome by showing kindness to a man who would surely be set free. Either reason is a possible answer as to why Paul's friends were allowed to accompany him.

A Mark of Brotherly Love

That Luke and Aristarchus were with Paul is an indication of their love for him. Luke and Aristarchus were not taking a cruise with some friends to Honolulu. They were headed toward Rome knowing that they awaited the same fate as Paul. The threat of losing life and limb didn't bother them because of their love for God and their affection for the apostle.

A godly leader has people who not only follow him but also love him. Luke and Aristarchus loved Paul to the point where they were willing to sacrifice their own lives for the sake of their ministry to him.

2. The prisoners (v. 1c)

"They delivered Paul and certain other prisoners unto one named Julius, a centurion of Augustus' band."

A group of prisoners—including Paul—had been quartered at Caesarea for some time and now were to be taken to Rome. Some were to be tried, others sentenced, and others executed.

a) The duties of centurions

All the prisoners were placed under the charge of Julius, "a centurion of Augustus' band." A centurion commanded one hundred men. "Augustus" was a title for the emperor of Rome. Augustus's band was a special cohort of men assigned to protect the emperor and carry out any special request he might have.

When the Roman government began to send its troops throughout the Empire, certain men were assigned to accompany the food rations. They were responsible for the safe transportation of the food to and from its destination. As time went on, those special couriers became sophisticated imperial agents responsible for transporting and spying on political prisoners. Julius commanded one hundred of those men, although it is uncertain exactly how many of them accompanied Paul on the ship. It is known that when the men later changed ships there was a total of 276 people (v. 37).

11

b) The integrity of centurions

The Romans were not adept at selecting governors because of the political maneuvering involved, but they were usually very good at picking leaders for their armies. Several passages in Scripture show that centurions tended to be men of integrity (e.g., Luke 7:1-10; Acts 10:1-2; 22:25-26).

3. The port (v. 2*a*)

"Entering into a ship of Adramyttium, we put to sea, meaning to sail by the coasts of Asia."

Adramyttium was the port where their ship was registered. Since it was a coastal vessel, the ship hugged the coastline and rarely ventured out into the open sea. The ship was on its way back to Adramyttium.

There were several kinds of ships in those days. There were those that ventured into the open sea and others that sailed from coast to coast and from one port to the next. In this case the intent was to go from port to port, as they hoped to connect with a ship that was on the way to Rome on which to put Paul and his fellow prisoners. Since there were no passenger ships, they had to rely on transport vessels.

4. The permission (v. 3)

"The next day we touched at Sidon. And Julius courteously treated Paul, and gave him liberty to go unto his friends to refresh himself."

Since Paul was a prisoner, it's not likely that he and Julius were friends. The Romans had very strict rules concerning their prisoners. If a Roman soldier lost a prisoner, he served the prisoner's sentence himself—regardless of the circumstances. Commander Julius must have had a very good reason for allowing Paul liberty to go ashore and meet with his friends. It is likely that Governor Festus informed Julius of Paul's innocence and assured him that Paul would in no way jeopardize his command.

a) The church at Sidon

Apparently there was a group of believers in Sidon. That they were called "friends" is not unusual. Jesus said, "I call you not servants; for the servant knoweth not what his lord doeth: but I have called you friends" (John 15:15). It was a common term used by the early church to designate other Christians.

The church at Sidon apparently came about as a result of repercussions from the persecution of Stephen. When Stephen was martyred, the church was scattered throughout the area of Judea and Samaria, including the areas of Sidon and Tyre (Acts 8:1; 11:19). Paul had visited that church on his way to Jerusalem (Acts 20:4-14) and now was visiting it again.

b) The refreshment of Paul

What did Paul do when he arrived at Sidon? No doubt he enjoyed the fellowship of the church and did some teaching and ministering simply because that was his nature. However the predominant reason Paul went was "to refresh himself." The Greek word translated "refresh" (*epimelēias*) is a medical term, which indicates that Paul was sick. That is not surprising considering that he had been a prisoner for two years. He was probably not able to get the diet, rest, and care he needed on the ship, so Julius allowed the believers in Sidon to minister to him.

5. The problems (v. 4)

"When we had put to sea from there, we sailed under the lee of Cyprus, because the winds were contrary."

a) The winds

The normal route would not have been to go around Cyprus, but because the wind was such a problem they had to sail close to the coast. Since this was a coastal vessel, it wouldn't dare venture into the open sea if there was any hint of wind problems. By travel-

13

ing close to the coast, they could take advantage of the land and the winds breaking at the shore.

b) The weather

This journey probably took place in the late summer months. Since the winds were westerly in the summer, the ship could easily tack against them and make good progress toward Rome. But mid-August was getting near the treacherous season, which ran from September 14 through November 11, according to Bible scholar F. F. Bruce (*Commentary on the Book of Acts* [Grand Rapids: Eerdmans, 1975], p. 506). No one dared cross the Mediterranean then. The winds were strong, and the sea was very rough at that time, so virtually all shipping ceased during that period.

6. The pilgrimage (vv. 5-6)

a) The ship's origin (v. 5)

"When we had sailed over the sea of Cilicia and Pamphylia, we came to Myra, a city of Lycia."

Paul knew that area well. He had been born and reared in the area surrounding Cilicia and had taken three missionary journeys to that territory. Myra was actually two miles inland but was known as the harbor town itself. It was the southernmost region of Asia Minor and was a chief port for Egyptian vessels passing through the area.

Egypt was the granary of the Roman Empire. The imperial government had a fleet that carried grain to the various places it was needed. When the ships came from Alexandria—the main port of Egypt—they dispensed the grain needed in the area of Asia Minor at the port of Myra. They often harbored there in difficult weather until they could proceed farther west to Italy.

b) The centurion's opportunity (v. 6)

"There the centurion found a ship of Alexandria sailing into Italy; and he put us on board."

When they arrived in Myra, a grain ship headed back to Rome happened to be there. The transfer was made, and the ship now had a total of 276 people, a good percentage consisting of Paul and the other prisoners. Historians have indicated that it would have taken approximately nine days to travel from Sidon to Myra. After the seamen had tacked back and forth against the coast for nine days, Myra would have been a welcome sight. It was a popular harbor, and Paul would have been glad to get there.

7. The slow progress (vv. 7-8)

a) The danger (v. 7)

"When we had sailed slowly many days, and scarcely were come off Cnidus, the wind not permitting us, we sailed under the lee of Crete, off Salmone."

They left Myra and very slowly sailed west between Rhodes and the mainland of Asia Minor. When they had passed Cnidus, they immediately left the shelter of land. The gentle land winds, which had provided protection, now ceased, and the open sea winds became very strong. As a result, they were unable to harbor at Cnidus. They ran directly into the prevailing wind and headwaters, so the only thing they could do was try to get the ship under the protecting shelter of Crete to hide from the wind.

Roman transportation ships were heavy and would have displaced a tremendous amount of water. Since they were grain ships, they were loaded down. Each had a single mast with a large, square sail, and the seamen usually preferred to navigate with that sail behind the wind. But when the wind was gusting heavily, such grain ships were hard to handle. During this journey, the wind prevented them from going to either of Cnidus's two harbors. Instead, they had to sail around the treacherous cape at Salmone to reach the shelter of the back side of Crete. Once they got around the cape, they would be secure from the hazardous northwesterly wind.

b) The difficulty (v. 8)

"And passing it with difficulty, came unto a place which is called Fair Havens, near to which was the city of Lasea."

They did not have an easy time going around Cape Salmone, which was on the eastern tip of Crete, because Crete is a 140-mile-long island. They finally arrived at a place called Fair Havens (Gk., *kalos limeōnas*), near the city of Lasea.

B. The Stay (vv. 9-12)

1. Paul's concern about the voyage (vv. 9-10)

The men aboard ship took on supplies and were eager to go on to Rome before winter came. If they didn't get to Rome before winter set in, the shipowner would have to take care of the entire crew for the three to four months of winter. To be stuck in Fair Havens would have been very undesirable because it was exposed to the winds of the open sea (v. 12).

The captain knew that to make money on the cargo he was carrying, it had to reach its destination as soon as possible. He didn't want to spend the entire winter paying his crew for idleness. Therefore he was willing to gamble on their making it to Rome.

a) The weather (v. 9*a*)

"When much time was spent, and when sailing was now dangerous."

It is not known how much time was spent in Fair Havens, but it must have been at least a month. If they

16

arrived sometime in mid-August, it would now be about mid-September. That would have been right at the beginning of the treacherous season running from September 14 through November 11.

b) The timing (v. 9b)

"Because the fast was already passed."

"The fast" is a reference to the Jewish Day of Atonement, commonly called "Yom Kippur." It occurs on the tenth day of Tishri, which is the seventh month in the Jewish calendar. That would put their journey at the end of September or the beginning of October. In A.D. 59, one of the dates proposed for Festus's short term of office, Yom Kippur occurred on October 5, and if the journey occurred after that, it would have been well into the dangerous season for sailing. Any attempt to sail at that time would have been a gamble.

c) The warning (vv. 9c-10)

"Paul admonished them, and said unto them, Sirs, I perceive that this voyage will be with injury and much damage, not only of the cargo and ship, but also of our lives."

Paul was not a sailor but had apparently been in shipwrecks before (2 Cor. 11:25), and didn't want to go through another. He was attempting to give them some practical advice so that a shipwreck wouldn't occur. He didn't say they would all die, but he did say the voyage would be disastrous. One of the qualities of a true spiritual leader is that he is a very practical man.

2. The centurion's choice to go on (vv. 11-12)

a) The men in charge (v. 11)

"Nevertheless, the centurion believed the master and the owner of the ship, more than those things which were spoken by Paul."

17

The words "master" and "owner" are difficult to translate from the Greek text because they do not occur often in the New Testament. The best translation of "master" seems to be "sailing master" or "pilot." He was responsible for navigating the ship. "Owner" should be translated "captain." In some cases the captain was also the owner if it was a private vessel, but since this was an imperial vessel, he would have been simply the captain.

b) The majority who chose (v. 12)

"Because the haven was not commodious to winter in, the greater part advised to depart from there also, if by any means they might attain to Phoenicia [Phoenix], and there to winter; which is an haven of Crete, and lieth toward the southwest and northwest."

The centurion agreed with the pilot and captain as did the majority of those on the ship. It is difficult to blame them, because the pilot and the captain were experts on weather and navigation. Their main reason for wanting to continue on to Rome was that Fair Havens was not a desirable place to stay. Historians record that the only place that was comfortable in the winter season was the port of Phoenix, which was about forty miles from Fair Havens. It was located between the southwest and northwest side of the island.

C. The Storm (vv. 13-26)

1. The deceptive breezes (v. 13)

"When the south wind blew softly, supposing that they had obtained their purpose, loosing from there, they sailed close by Crete."

It must have been a very deceptive thing for the crew when the wind began to blow softly. They assumed that the winds would simply carry them right on course, and, if not, they would at least be able to winter at Phoenix.

2. The destructive tempest (v. 14)

"But not long after there arose against it a tempestuous wind, called Euroclydon."

Euroclydon, or *Euraquilo* as it is called in the textual margin, was a sailor's term for a strong northeasterly wind. It came from two words—one Greek and one Latin. The Greek word *euros* refers to an east wind, and the Latin word *aquilo* to a north wind. This northeast wind came down from Asia Minor and was so fierce as to be of hurricane proportions. The gentle south wind that had carried them along was now replaced by a treacherous, deadly northeasterly wind. They were bobbing up and down, being tumbled about and beaten by the wind. The Euroclydon was greatly feared among all who sailed the Mediterranean because it tended to send ships to an ocean graveyard off the coast of North Africa. Archaeologists have discovered the remains of many ships there.

3. The driven ship (v. 15-17)

a) Looking for protection (vv. 15-16*a*)

"When the ship was caught, and could not bear up into the wind, we let her drive. And running under the lee of a certain island which is called Clauda."

The Euroclydon didn't capsize the ship but began to drive it south, because the wind was blowing from the northeast. They started at Fair Havens and twenty-three miles later were near a small island called Clauda. They tried with great effort to get behind the island to gain some protection from the tempest.

b) Preparing the ship (vv. 16*b*-17)

(1) They secured the lifeboat (v. 16*b*)

"We had much work to secure the boat."

Every sailing vessel had a dinghy. When the vessel was harbored, the dinghy could be used as transportation to go ashore. It could also be used as a lifeboat in case the ship was destroyed. Normally the dinghy was attached to the stern of the ship by a rope and simply pulled along. But if stormy weather occurred, the crew had to secure the lifeboat or it would fill with water, drag, and eventually snap the rope. With great difficulty everyone worked to secure the lifeboat.

(2) They undergirded the ship (v. 17a)

"When they had hoisted it [the lifeboat], they used helps, undergirding the ship."

In those days shipbuilders couldn't bolt the planks to the girders because they didn't have bolts. The only way they could secure a ship was to tie or glue it. In a single-masted vessel there was no distribution of stress, as opposed to a multi-sail vessel, where the stress is distributed over the entire hull. The ship would simply begin to split in half. The sailors would attempt to wrap cables tightly around the ship to keep it secured during a storm, a procedure called "frapping" (Albert Barnes, *Notes on the New Testament: Acts* [Grand Rapids: Baker, 1975], p. 364).

(3) They struck the sail (v. 17b)

"Fearing lest they should fall into the quicksands, struck sail, and so were driven."

The Greek word translated "quicksand" is *surtis* and refers to the reef or sandbar that was so treacherous to ships in that area. Albert Barnes tells us "there were two celebrated *syrtes*, or quicksands, on the coast of Africa, called the greater and lesser. They were vast beds of sand driven up by the sea, and constantly shifting their position, so that it could not be known certainly where the danger was" (p. 354).

It wouldn't have done any good for the crew to keep up the sail, because the ship would have torn apart. Therefore they dropped the sail and allowed themselves to be driven by the waves and the wind. With the sail down, the storm swirling around them from all sides, and the seamen unable to navigate, God caused them to sail on a direct course to the harbor of Malta.

4. The desperate measures (vv. 18-20)

   a) Lightening the load (v. 18)

   "We being exceedingly tossed with a tempest, the next day they lightened the ship."

   The next day they jettisoned part of the cargo (cf. Jonah 1:5). They kept some for ballast, some for their own food, and some, it was hoped, for their eventual arrival in Rome.

   b) Casting the tackle (v. 19)

   "The third day we cast out with our own hands the tackle of the ship."

   Verse 18 says "they" lightened the ship, whereas verse 19 says, "We cast out with our own hands the tackle of the ship." The situation became so desperate that the entire group—crew and prisoners—began throwing overboard the excess tackle, such as unnecessary sails, cables, furniture, and baggage. They had been only three days off the coast of Fair Havens and already had to jettison cargo and tackle.

   c) Abandoning hope (v. 20)

   "When neither sun nor stars in many days appeared, and no small tempest lay on us, all hope that we should be saved was then taken away."

   The men on the ship lost all hope. They had nothing and no one to turn to. But that is exactly what God wanted.

5. The divine comfort (vv. 21-26)

   a) The lack of food (v. 21)

   "But after being long without food."

   Because of seasickness and contamination of the food by the salt water, no one had eaten in a long time. Since they had jettisoned their cargo, they had only a limited supply. And they must have been much too busy to eat, because their lives had been in constant danger.

   b) The failure to listen (v. 21*b*)

   "Paul stood forth in the midst of them, and said, Sirs, ye should have hearkened unto me, and not have loosed from Crete, and to have gained this harm and loss."

   Paul could not resist an "I told you so." He reminded captain and crew that what he had said had come to pass, thus establishing his credibility as God's representative.

   c) The preservation of life (v. 22)

   "Now I exhort you to be of good cheer; for there shall be no loss of any man's life among you, but only of the ship."

   "Be of good cheer" must have seemed a ridiculous statement considering the circumstances. The ship was teetering back and forth, waves were smashing the top of the mast, and visibility was almost zero. But Paul gave a reason for his statement: "There shall be no loss of any man's life among you, but only of the ship." The crew was probably saying, "Terrific! And when that happens, we'll just walk on the water, right?" Why would they believe Paul? Maybe because of their present situation. God had authenticated Paul's credibility, and now the foundation was established for the crew to believe him in the future.

d) The trustworthiness of God (vv. 23-26)

"There stood by me this night an angel of God, whose I am, and whom I serve, saying, Fear not, Paul, thou must be brought before Caesar; and, lo, God hath given thee all them that sail with thee. Wherefore, sirs, be of good cheer; for I believe God, that it shall be even as it was told me. However, we must be cast upon a certain island."

Paul made sure that God was the focus of the situation. God introduced Himself to these men by getting them into a desperate position. And because they sensed imminent death, they looked for God. They knew only God could help them in this situation.

By communicating his vision of the angel, Paul was putting himself out on a limb: if what he said didn't come true, his vision wasn't from God. Do you realize the likelihood of landing on the only island around, losing ship and cargo, and yet everyone's life being saved? The mathematical improbability of that occurring would be staggering. It would not be surprising, however, if God engineered every detail to fit His plan. And He did!

How God's People Protect Society

Acts 27:24 reminds us that God's people—in the midst of an ungodly society—actually act as a protection to the community. That principle is clear in Scripture.

1. Genesis 18:32—Abraham said, "Let not the Lord be angry, and I will speak yet but this once: Suppose ten shall be found there [Sodom]. And he [God] said, I will not destroy it for ten's sake." God was prepared to spare the entire city to save the righteous people who lived in it. Unfortunately there weren't ten righteous people living in the city. The principle, however, holds true. The righteous act as a protection for the unrighteous.

2. Genesis 30:27—Laban told Jacob, "I pray thee, if I have found favor in thine eyes, tarry; for I have learned by experience that

the Lord hath blessed me for thy sake." Laban recognized that the blessing of God fell upon him when Jacob was present.

3. Genesis 39:5—"From the time that he [Potiphar] had made him [Joseph] overseer in his house, and over all that he had, that the Lord blessed the Egyptian's house for Joseph's sake; and the blessing of the Lord was upon all that he had in the house, and in the field."

The world doesn't know how fortunate it is to have godly people in its midst. The men on board the ship carrying the apostle Paul didn't know how fortunate they were to have him present.

Focusing on the Facts

1. Why have archaeologists and historians been interested in Acts 27 (see p. 8)?
2. What does Acts 27 tell us about God's providence (see p. 9)?
3. The true mettle of a person shines forth in the _____ of _____ (see p. 9).
4. To whom does the "we" in Acts 27:1 refer (see p. 10)?
5. Describe two theories that would explain why Paul was allowed to have companions on his journey to Rome (see p. 10).
6. Describe the centurion's duty and the origin of Augustus's band (see p. 11).
7. Why was Paul's liberty to leave the ship such an unusual occurrence (see p. 12)?
8. What was the origin of the church at Sidon? Why did Paul go there (see p. 13)?
9. When was the treacherous season on the open sea (see p. 14)?
10. What link did Egypt have with the Roman Empire (see p. 14)?
11. Why was Fair Havens not a good place to stay for the winter (Acts 27:12; see p. 16)?
12. What was the captain's motive in wanting to leave Fair Havens (see p. 16)?
13. To which fast does Acts 27:9 refer (see p. 17)?
14. One of the qualities of a true spiritual leader is that he is a very _____ man (see p. 17).
15. Who were the men in charge of the ship carrying Paul (Acts 27:11; see pp. 17-18)?
16. What was the Euroclydon (see p. 19)?

17. What did the crew and passengers struggle to do during the storm (Acts 27:18-19; see p. 21)?
18. Why did men on the ship give up hope (v. 20; see p. 21)?
19. Why did Paul tell the crew they should have listened to him (see p. 22)?
20. What principle can be seen in the sentence "God hath given thee all them that sail with thee" (Acts 27:24)? Support your answer with Scripture (see pp. 23-24).

Pondering the Principles

1. God was in complete control of all that happened to the apostle Paul. None of the events or elements was outside the sovereign control of God. Do you believe that every event in your life is under His control? Study the following verses and thank God for His sovereignty: Psalm 103:19; Daniel 4:24-25, 34-35; Acts 17:24-28.

2. Luke and Aristarchus were committed to Paul because he was committed to God. They were headed for Rome knowing that they awaited the same fate as Paul. Because of their love for God and their affection for Paul, the threat of losing their lives was inconsequential. Are you willing to love God regardless of the circumstances? How would you have responded if you were Joseph in Genesis 37? After reading the following chapters about Joseph's life in slavery, read Genesis 45:5-8, and ask God to give you the same kind of attitude in your present circumstances.

2
Paul's Journey to Rome—Part 2

Outline

Introduction

Review
I. The Passage
  A. The Start (vv. 1-8)
  B. The Stay (vv. 9-12)
  C. The Storm (vv. 13-26)

Lesson
  D. The Shipwreck (vv. 27-41)
    1. The calculations of the crew (vv. 27-28)
      a) Reconstructing the distance (v. 27)
      b) Sounding the depths (v. 28)
    2. The fear of the crew (vv. 29-30)
      a) Their plan (v. 29)
      b) Their panic (v. 30)
    3. The foiling of the plot (vv. 31-32)
      a) The wisdom of Paul (v. 31)
      b) The decision of the centurion (v. 32)
    4. The encouragement from Paul (vv. 33-35)
      a) Strength (v. 33)
      b) Safety (v. 34)
      c) Service (v. 35)
    5. The good cheer of the passengers and crew (vv. 36-37)
    6. The lightening of the ship (v. 38)
    7. The destruction of the ship (vv. 39-41)
      a) Sailing into a creek (v. 39)
      b) Making toward shore (v. 40)
      c) Running the ship aground (v. 41)

Introduction

Acts 27 describes one of the shipwrecks the apostle Paul experienced. Also it illustrates leadership in crisis. It describes a man who experienced a tremendously stressful situation, demonstrating all the abilities any great leader must possess.

Review

I. THE PASSAGE

  A. The Start (vv. 1-8; see pp. 9-16)

  B. The Stay (vv. 9-12; see pp. 16-18)

C. The Storm (vv. 13-26; see pp. 18-23)

As the ship continued to be driven by the storm, the struggle to stay afloat caused the crew and prisoners to neglect eating for two weeks. They didn't know where they were or which direction they were going. In the midst of the storm, they were without hope of ever being saved. Nevertheless, with God's credibility at stake, Paul assured the men that they would be saved (v. 24.)

Lesson

D. The Shipwreck (vv. 27-41)

1. The calculations of the crew (vv. 27-28)

a) Reconstructing the distance (v. 27)

"When the fourteenth night was come, as we were driven up and down in Adria, about midnight the sailors deemed that they drew near to some country."

Fourteen days had passed since they left Fair Havens in Crete, and now they were being driven about Adria, the center of the Mediterranean Sea. That was the only knowledge they had regarding their whereabouts. "Driven up and down" gives the idea that they had no idea which direction they were going. At midnight the sailors sensed they were approaching land, perhaps because they could hear the sound of the surf pounding on the shore.

The distance from Clauda, their last known destination, to Malta, where they ended up, is about 470 miles. Mediterranean navigators have indicated that such a ship in a windstorm would drift approximately thirty-six miles every twenty-four hours (F. F. Bruce, *Commentary on the Book of Acts* [Grand Rapids: Eerdmans, 1975], p. 514). It would therefore have taken them about thirteen days to be driven from Clauda to Malta. And if you add one day to account for travel from Fair Havens to Clauda, you come up with exactly fourteen days of travel (v. 27). Navigational information corroborates the biblical text.

Since the ship had already been fourteen days on the open sea, it was probably only a few miles from the entrance of the harbor at Malta. That harbor has been renamed St. Paul's Harbor.

b) Sounding the depths (v. 28)

"[They] sounded, and found it twenty fathoms; and when they had gone a little farther, they sounded again, and found it fifteen fathoms."

To verify that they were approaching land, they dropped a line with a leaded weight into the sea to determine the depth. They found they were at twenty fathoms (120 feet). A little later they verified that the water was getting more shallow.

2. The fear of the crew (vv. 29-30)

a) Their plan (v. 29)

"Fearing lest we should fall upon rocks, they cast four anchors out of the stern, and wished for the day."

Since they were in the black of night and unable to see, they were in danger of hitting the coastline. That was cause for panic, so they dropped four anchors from the stern. Since they anchored the stern, the driving force of the storm kept the bow pointed toward the shore. They eagerly awaited daybreak so that they could see how close land was, cut the four anchors, and be driven onto land.

b) Their panic (v. 30)

"As the sailors were about to flee out of the ship, when they had let down the boat into the sea, under pretense as though they would have cast anchors out of the foreship."

The crew was so panicked they were going to abandon ship in complete darkness, in the middle of a storm, and then try to make it to shore in a dinghy. They had no idea where the shore was and didn't even know what was on the shore itself. Perhaps they thought it would be better to hit the rocks in a dinghy than in a lumbering ship. They tried to make it appear as though they were dropping anchors over the bow but were actually dropping the dinghy into the water.

3. The foiling of the plot (vv. 31-32)

   a) The wisdom of Paul (v. 31)

   "Paul said to the centurion and to the soldiers, except these abide in the ship, ye cannot be saved."

   Their irrational plot did not work, because Paul was alert and caught them. God wanted everyone on that ship saved. Going through the proper chain of command, he notified the centurion. By this time, the centurion was willing to believe anything Paul said because everything else he said had come to pass. Also it would have been disastrous for the whole crew to abandon ship because there would have been no skilled seamen left to take the ship safely to shore when daybreak came.

   b) The decision of the centurion (v. 32)

   "The soldiers cut off the ropes of the boat, and let her fall off."

   The centurion heeded Paul's words but then went one step further: he commanded the soldiers to cut the ropes holding the dinghy and let it fall into the water. They could have used it to get to shore later but now would have to swim. The centurion must have believed cutting away the dinghy was the only way to stop the crew.

4. The encouragement from Paul (vv. 33-35)

 a) Strength (v. 33)

"Paul besought them all to take food, saying, This day is the fourteenth day that ye have tarried and continued fasting, having taken nothing."

In a sense, Paul was now in command. Everyone was looking to him for the next instructions. He urged them all to eat—since they had not eaten in fourteen days. They would need energy for the hard work that lay ahead. If they ever expected to get to land, they were going to have to regain their strength.

 b) Safety (v. 34)

"I beseech you to take some food; for this is for your health; for there shall not an hair fall from the head of any of you."

The Greek word translated "health" (*sōterias*) means "deliverance," "preservation," or "safety." In Scripture it refers to both physical deliverance and spiritual salvation, but here it simply refers to physical well-being or safety.

"There shall not an hair fall from the head of any of you" is an old Jewish proverb that refers to safety and security (1 Sam. 14:45; 2 Sam. 14:11; 1 Kings 1:52; Luke 21:18).

 c) Service (v. 35)

"When he had thus spoken, he took bread, and gave thanks to God in the presence of them all; and when he had broken it, he began to eat."

Here are two great keys to serving the Lord—prayer and a good breakfast! It's a balanced meal of spiritual guidance and physical nourishment. Since Paul assured them that everyone would survive the shipwreck, there was no excuse not to have a good breakfast. Here we see the balance between the sovereignty of God and the responsibility of man: it was God's responsibility to save the people and Paul's responsibility to have everyone eat and be strengthened. By eating first, Paul set the example for the others to trust God and then eat.

5. The good cheer of the passengers and crew (vv. 36-37)

"Then were they all of good cheer, and they also took some food. And we were in all in the ship two hundred and seventy-six souls."

Everyone was so captivated by Paul's courage that they too began to eat and have hope.

6. The lightening of the ship (v. 38)

"When they had eaten enough, they lightened the ship, and cast out the wheat into the sea."

They had already jettisoned a great deal of cargo (vv. 10, 18-19) but kept some for ballast. By this time any cargo would have been unnecessary because they now planned to beach the ship and needed it to be as light as possible. Most of the cargo had probably been soaked with saltwater anyway.

7. The destruction of the ship (vv. 39-41)

a) Sailing into a creek (v. 39)

"When it was day, they recognized not the land; but they discovered a certain creek with a shore, into which they were minded, if it were possible, to thrust in the ship."

The day dawned, and they saw land but still didn't know where they were. The "creek with a shore" most likely refers to a beach that comes off the island of Malta and empties into the bay. Their intention was to head for the creek and run aground on the beach.

b) Making toward shore (v. 40)

"When they had taken up [cast off] the anchors, they committed themselves unto the sea, and loosed the rudder bands, and hoisted up the mainsail to the wind, and made toward shore."

They allowed themselves to be driven by the wind and sea. They loosed the undergirding they had used to tighten the ship earlier (v. 17) to give some measure of steering and then hoisted the mainsail so that the wind would drive them toward shore.

c) Running the ship aground (v. 41)

"Falling into a place where two seas met, they ran the ship aground; and the bow stuck fast and remained unmoveable, but the stern was broken with the violence of the waves."

"A place where two seas met" (Gk., *dithalasson*) is difficult to translate. It could refer to a shoal or reef. Also, in the middle of the bay there is a small island called Salmonetta, which intersects with the island of Malta to form a sandbank between two currents. Perhaps the ship got stuck on that sandbar. They may have assumed the island was an extension of the mainland. The bow stuck in the sandbar a good distance from shore, and with the waves smashing against the stern, the ship was dashed to pieces.

E. The Safety (vv. 42-44)

1. The counsel (v. 42)

"The soldiers' counsel was to kill the prisoners, lest any of them should swim out and escape."

The soldiers were afraid of losing their lives in the shipwreck, but they were equally afraid that their prisoners would escape. The traditional Roman discipline was that any soldier who allowed his prisoner to escape was responsible for serving out that prisoner's sentence. The soldiers wanted to kill Paul and the rest of the prisoners to prevent that from happening.

2. The commandment (vv. 43-44*a*)

"But the centurion, willing to save Paul, kept them from their purpose, and commanded that they who could swim should cast themselves first into the sea, and get to land; and the rest, some on boards, and some on broken pieces of the ship."

The centurion rushed in at that point to save Paul and the other prisoners from a violent death. The prisoners should have been eternally grateful to Paul for being in their midst, because without him the centurion might have granted the soldiers' request for their execution. The centurion's command was for everyone to jump into the water and swim to shore. Those who couldn't swim were to cling to floating debris and eventually make their way to land.

3. The confirmation (v. 44*b*)

"And so it came to pass that they all escaped safely to the land."

Two hundred seventy-six men jumped into the water, and 276 people met on the shore! The first thought those men must have had was that the God Paul worshiped was faithful to His word. God not only established His own veracity but also established the credibility of the apostle Paul. Over and over again, God has kept His word.

a) Isaiah 40:8—"The grass withereth, the flower fadeth, but the word of our God shall stand forever" (cf. 1 Pet. 1:25).

b) Isaiah 55:10-11—The Lord said, "As the rain cometh down, and the snow from heaven, and returneth not there, but watereth the earth, and maketh it bring forth and bud, that it may give seed to the sower, and bread to the eater, so shall my word be that goeth forth out of my mouth; it shall not return unto me void, but it shall accomplish that which I please, and it shall prosper in the thing whereto I sent it." God's Word always will be fulfilled.

c) Matthew 5:18—Jesus said, "Verily I say unto you, Till heaven and earth pass, one jot or one tittle shall in no way pass from the law, till all be fulfilled." God's Word is reliable.

d) John 17:17—Jesus said to the Father, "Thy word is truth."

God allowed each person on the ship to see that He was in complete, sovereign control. As He has done so often in the history of His revelation to mankind, He used predictive prophecy to establish His divine authority. When He says something will happen and it does, God is proved to be who He claims to be. One of the greatest proofs that God is the Author of the Bible is the fulfillment of prophecy. Some of those prophecies, such as the ones recorded in this passage, have been fulfilled and some are being fulfilled today, that the convincing may go on.

II. THE PRINCIPLES

Acts 27 describes true spiritual leadership exemplified in the life of Paul. But what specific qualities enabled him to be such a dynamic leader?

A. A Godly Leader Is Loved

A godly leader is loved. This isn't always true in the world; it is always true in the church. True spiritual leadership does not mean you will be loved by everyone at all times. But it does mean that a man who leads for God will be beloved because of his integrity. In verse 3 we saw that Julius allowed Paul to go to the believers in Sidon and refresh himself. Paul primarily taught doctrine and was involved in many spiritual matters, but he went to them for his physical needs. Because they loved and appreciated all he had done for them, they were happy to serve him in that way.

Some people assume that to be a strong leader you must eliminate people's love for you. They think that to be a leader, you must do away with any hint of vulnerability, because it shows you are weak. That is not true! Godly leaders are loved because they lead with care, humility, and approachability (1 Pet. 5:1-5). If you are not leading in that way, you are not being led by the Holy Spirit, who generates in the hearts of people a love for their leaders. Though church leaders aren't perfect, there must be an irresistible quality that makes them easy to love.

1. Titus 3:15—Paul told Titus, "All that are with me greet thee. Greet them that love us in the faith." Paul knew that people loved him, even though he was a disciplinarian. When something needed to be said, he stated it in no uncertain terms, even to the apostle Peter (Gal. 2:11). When there was an issue to be dealt with, he dealt with it in a strong and firm way but was no less loving. In spite of his failures, there was an irresistible quality that made him lovable. Jesus, the strongest leader who ever lived, was so loved that words cannot express that love.

2. 1 Corinthians 13:1—Paul said, "Though I speak with the tongues of men and of angels, and have not love, I am become as sounding bronze, or a tinkling cymbal."

3. 1 Timothy 4:12—Paul told Timothy, "Be thou an example . . . in love."

4. 1 Timothy 6:11—Paul also said, "Thou, O man of God . . . follow after love."

B. A Godly Leader Never Quits

Paul was suffering from sickness yet still pursued his objectives. If he was sick in Sidon, you can imagine what he must have felt like on board ship. He had been fourteen days without food, fighting the storm, yet he never quit. And that doesn't count his other shipwrecks and hardships (2 Cor. 11:24-33).

From a human standpoint, you have to wonder how Paul could go through imprisonment, trials, murder plots, sickness, and shipwrecks and yet not want to quit. The physical pain alone would have been too much for almost anyone to endure. He simply didn't know the meaning of the word *quit*. It's been rightly said, "When the going gets tough, the tough get going," and, "It isn't the size of the man in the fight, but the size of the fight in the man." Paul was that kind of a man.

C. A Godly Leader Uses Good Judgment

True leaders make practical, wise decisions. While they were in Fair Havens, it was the dangerous season for sailing, and Paul knew it was not wise to leave port (vv. 9-10). Paul knew God wanted him in Rome (cf. Acts 23:11) but never lost his sense of practicality. He never became foolish or presumed on God but trusted Him to work out His will at the best time.

1. Psalm 19:13—King David said, "Keep back thy servant also from presumptuous sins."

2. Matthew 4:8-10—The devil tempted Jesus to sin when he took "him up into an exceedingly high mountain, and showeth him all the kingdoms of the world, and the glory of them, and saith unto him, All these things will I give thee, if thou wilt fall down and worship me. Then saith Jesus unto him, Begone, Satan; for it is written, Thou shalt worship the Lord, thy God, and him only shalt thou serve."

Jesus the Messiah knew He would ultimately inherit the kingdoms of the world. But Satan thought he could seduce Jesus into presuming on God and taking them ahead of schedule. Christ elected to wait on God's timetable. In other temptations Satan tempted Him to jump ahead of God (vv. 3-7). But Jesus could not be forced to presume on something that had already been promised Him at the right time.

Many people presume on God to the point where they mislead others. Many pastors have got into monumental building programs, spending large amounts of money, and then are caught breaking the law. They assume the end justifies the means. In the end they lose their sense of sanity and practicality. What they need to do is allow God to accomplish what He wants in His own time.

D. A Godly Leader Speaks with Authority

Paul knew what he was talking about. He said, "I exhort you to be of good cheer; for there shall be no loss of any man's life among you, but only of the ship. For there stood by me this night an angel of God, whose I am, and whom I serve, saying, Fear not, Paul, thou must be brought before Caesar; and, lo, God hath given thee all them that sail with thee. Wherefore, sirs, be of good cheer; for I believe God, that it shall be even as it was told me" (vv. 22-25).

Paul spoke with extreme boldness. A leader must speak with authority. And his authority comes not from himself but from the Word of God. James Montgomery Boice, pastor of the historic Tenth Presbyterian Church in Philadelphia, said, "What is required of the minister? Clearly the first and essential requirement is a joyful and total commitment to the absolute authority of God's written revelation. . . . Since belief in the Scriptures as the infallible and authoritative Word of God has declined in the life of the Church generally, it is not surprising that the eloquence and power of the proclamation of this Word have diminished also. What is the result? It is well put in this description of a panel discussion involving a rabbi, a priest, and a Protestant minister. The rabbi stood up and said, 'I speak according to the law of Moses.' The priest said, 'I speak according to the Church.' The clergyman rose to his feet and said, 'It seems to me....' " ("The Great Need for Preaching," *Christianity Today* [20 Dec. 1974]: 7-9).

Unfortunately, that is what is happening in Christianity today. But the true spiritual leader knows the Bible and stands on its authority. There would have been no comfort for the crew if Paul had said, "Well, fellows, it seems to me that we just might make it"! True spiritual leadership is authoritative.

E. A Godly Leader Strengthens Others

When Paul said, "Be of good cheer" (v. 25) and, "I beseech you to take some food" (v. 34), everyone was encouraged by his words (v. 36). A strong leader always strengthens others. We see that illustrated in 1 Samuel 30. First David was strengthened by God (v. 6), then he was able to strengthen others (vv. 9-10, 16-20).

F. A Godly Leader Has Unwavering Faith

Paul said, "I believe God." That was how he lived his life. Similarly Abraham "staggered not at the promise of God through unbelief, but was strong in faith, giving glory to God" (Rom. 4:20).

G. A Godly Leader Demands Obedience to God's Word

A true leader never compromises. Paul said, "Except these abide in the ship, ye cannot be saved" (v. 31). The crew tried to get away, but Paul in effect said, "You either do it God's way, or you will pay the consequences." The church is in desperate need of leaders who call people to obey God's Word.

H. A Godly Leader Leads by Example

When Paul wanted the men to eat, he ate first (vv. 34-35). Leadership by example is a common theme in the New Testament (e.g., 1 Pet. 5:3; Phil. 3:17; 4:9; 1 Thess. 1:5-6; 2 Thess. 3:6-9; 1 Tim. 4:12; Titus 2:7).

Conclusion

In addition to those features of leadership, we also see the promise that God will always fulfill His will. A leader knows the balance between God's absolute promise and his own responsibility. He knows God will fulfill His will, yet he remains practical and wise. He balances the sovereignty of God and his own practical efforts. He has a hearty breakfast but also prays for strength and guidance. This passage teaches the providence of God in protecting His leader, but we can also see the characteristics of true spiritual leadership. It is my prayer that should God place you in a leadership position, you will accept that responsibility—as Paul did—and manifest the characteristics of a truly godly leader.

Focusing on the Facts

1. What does Acts 27 illustrate (see p. 28)?
2. How does the historical, navigational information concerning the course of the ship corroborate the biblical text (see pp. 29-30)?
3. What does the term "sounding" mean in verse 28 (see p. 30)?
4. Why did the crew drop four anchors from the stern of the ship (v. 29)? What was their real intention (v. 30; see pp. 30-31)?
5. Why was Paul concerned that no man jump ship prematurely (vv. 31-32; see p. 31)?
6. Why did Paul encourage the men to eat? How long had it been since they had eaten (vv. 33-35; see p. 32)?
7. Describe the meaning of the old Jewish proverb that Paul refers to in verse 34. Use Scripture to support your answer (see p. 32).
8. Why did the crew jettison the rest of the cargo (v. 38; see p. 32)?
9. Explain the events leading up to and including the destruction of the ship (vv. 39-41; see pp. 33-34).
10. Why did the soldiers want to kill the prisoners (v. 42; see pp.34-35)?
11. How many of the passengers survived the shipwreck (v. 44; see p. 35)?
12. Give examples from Scriptures describing how God's Word can be trusted (see pp. 35-36).
13. One of the greatest proofs that God is the real Author of the Bible is the fulfillment of _____ (see p. 36).
14. True or false: To be a strong leader, you must eliminate people's love for you (see p. 37).
15. True leaders make _____, _____ decisions (see p. 38).
16. How did Jesus respond to Satan's ploys to get him to presume on God (Matt. 4:1-11; see p. 38)?
17. True or false: A leader's authority should come both from his own ingenuity and from the Word of God (see p. 39).
18. How did King David display his leadership abilities as recorded in 1 Samuel 30 (see p. 40)?

19. Leadership by _____ is a common theme in the New Testament (see p. 40).

Pondering the Principles

1. Godly leaders are loved by people because they show they care and are approachable. Are you a spiritual leader in your church, home, or family? Do those around you sense that you care for them? If not, take time right now and ask the Lord to make you the spiritual leader He wants you to be. Of the following verses, commit one to memory and ask God to make it a part of your leadership abilities: Titus 3:15; 1 Corinthians 13:1; 1 Timothy 4:12; 1 Timothy 6:11.

2. Greatly lacking in the church today are leaders who speak with authority. A true spiritual leader knows the Bible and stands on its absolutes. As a spiritual leader, where does your authority come from? Does it come more from your own ingenuity or from the Word of God? Read 1 Corinthians 1:17; 2:1-5; and 2 Corinthians 4:2 and determine whether you are communicating the truth of God or something of your own devising.

3. One of the greatest keys to leadership is that it must be done by example. People will follow those who lead by example in both attitudes and actions. Do people desire to follow you because of the example you set? Read the following verses, and ask God to manifest in you the characteristics of a godly leader: 1 Peter 5:3; Philippians 3:17; 2 Thessalonians 3:6-9.

3
The Last Lap

Outline

Introduction

Review

Lesson
 I. Pagan Hospitality (vv. 1-2)
    A. The Characteristics of Malta (v. 1)
       1. The topography of Malta
       2. The history of Malta
    B. The People of Malta (v. 2)
       1. Pagan kindness honored
          a) In Scripture
          b) In Malta
       2. Pagan kindness illustrated
       3. Pagan kindness explained
 II. Potential Harm (vv. 3-6)
    A. Paul's Humble Example (v. 3*a*)
       1. The example of Paul
       2. The example of Christ
    B. The Snake's Sudden Appearance (vv. 3*b*-4)
       1. Paul's predicament (v. 3*b*)
       2. The natives' assessment (v. 4)
    C. God's Miraculous Deliverance (vv. 5-6)
       1. A confirmation from God (v. 5)
       2. A change of opinion (v. 6)
 III. Public Healing (vv. 7-11)
    A. The Setting (v. 7)
       1. Publius's title (v. 7*a*)
       2. Publius's estate (v. 7*b*)
    B. The Problem (v. 8*a*)

Introduction

Acts 28:1-16 chronicles the events leading to Paul's arrival at Rome. Several years had passed since Paul first had the desire to go to Rome. Paul's reaction to his arrival is not recorded in Scripture, but perhaps in spirit he agreed with Psalm 107:29-30: "[God] maketh the storm a calm, so that the waves thereof are still. Then are they glad because they are quiet; so he bringeth them unto their desired haven." God fulfills the desires of His servants.

In Acts 27 we saw that Paul exemplified the qualities of a faithful leader. In this passage we will see God blessing His faithful servant. The narrative of the trip to Rome is rich because it gives us additional principles of leadership and also demonstrates the basis upon which God blesses faithful leaders.

Review

The last lap of Paul's journey began in Melita, or Malta as it is known today. His journey had already lasted two and a half months. Fourteen days he spent at sea as the crew of the ship that was carrying him to Rome fought against a terrible storm. They had no hope of being saved. They were unable to navigate because neither sun, moon, nor stars were visible. They arrived at Malta by God's providence as the bow of the ship stuck into a sandbar off-shore (Acts 27:41). As the waves beat against the stern, the ship began to disintegrate. At that point the soldiers planned to kill the prisoners so that they wouldn't escape (v. 42). However, the centurion, Julius, prevented them from doing that (v. 43). Ultimately all on board dove into the water. Some swam through the surf, while others clung to boards and debris (v. 44). Miraculously, all made it to shore. Earlier God had told Paul that the ship would be lost but everyone on board would be saved (v. 22). Everything God said came to pass. You can imagine that everyone from then on took Paul and the God he served very seriously.

So they arrived on the island of Malta, wet and exhausted. And they didn't know where they were.

Lesson

I. PAGAN HOSPITALITY (vv. 1-2)

Biblical Hospitality

One of the great virtues of Christianity is hospitality. It is to be characteristic of church elders (1 Tim. 3:2) and believers in general (1 Pet. 4:9). Hebrews 13:2 says, "Be not forgetful to entertain strangers; for thereby some have entertained angels unawares." For example, in the period before the destruction of Sodom and Gomorrah, Abraham and Sarah served dinner to three guests; as it turned out two of their visitors were angels and one was a preincarnate appearance of Christ (Gen. 18:1-15). Christians are to extend kindness toward strangers. Our homes are to be open and our lives available to meeting the needs of others.

1. Matthew 10:40-42—Jesus said, "He that receiveth you receiveth me, and he that receiveth me receiveth him that sent me. He that receiveth a prophet in the name of a prophet shall receive a prophet's reward; and he that receiveth a righteous man in the name of a righteous man shall receive a righteous man's reward. And whosoever shall give to drink unto one of these little ones a cup of cold water only in the name of a disciple, verily I say unto you, he shall in no way lose his reward." As the disciples went out to reach people for Christ, those who showed them hospitality would receive the blessing of God. God put a premium on hospitality, kindness, and gentleness toward strangers.

2. Luke 9:4-5—Jesus said, "Whatever house ye enter into, there abide, and from there depart. And whoever will not receive you, when ye go out of that city, shake off the very dust from your feet for a testimony against them." When the disciples were not shown hospitality, they were to treat the offenders as if they were Gentiles, which was a derogatory attitude to have toward a Jewish person.

3. Romans 12:13—Paul said, "Distributing to the necessity of saints; given to hospitality." Indeed, demonstrating hospitality is a necessity for all saints.

In Acts 28:1-2 we see the hospitality that the pagan people on Malta showed toward Paul and the others who were on the ship.

A. The Characteristics of Malta (v. 1)

"When they were escaped, then they knew that the island was called Melita."

1. The topography of Malta

They didn't recognize the island immediately because they came ashore by way of a bay now known as St. Paul's Bay. The main port of Malta is Valletta. It is likely that the sailors and soldiers had been to Malta before but didn't recognize this part of the island right away. But since the island is only about seventeen miles long and nine miles wide, it wouldn't have been long before they began to recognize features consistent with the topography of Malta. And surely the local people informed them where they were.

2. The history of Malta

The name "Melita" was given to the island by the ancient Phoenicians who came to the island from Palestine. They were great mariners, having charted much of the Mediterranean. Melita is a Phoenician word that means "refuge" or "escape." The island lies about sixty miles off the southern tip of Sicily. Since the early nineteenth century, it has been primarily dominated by the British but was granted full independence in 1964. Although English is the common language, the native Maltese language is a form of Arabic. That indicates Malta was established by people from the East, and it is believed that they were Phoenicians.

B. The People of Malta (v. 2)

"The barbarous people showed us no little kindness; for they kindled a fire, and received us, every one, because of the present rain, and because of the cold."

In mid-November the weather there would have been biting cold. The men were wet and exposed to the wind, so the natives prepared a fire for them.

The Greek word translated "barbarous" (*barbaros*) referred to anyone who spoke a non-Greek language. So Luke was indicating that the natives of Malta spoke a foreign language. It was not a derogatory term.

1. Pagan kindness honored

a) In Scripture

God takes note of the kindness that pagan people show to the children of God. In Genesis 12:2-3 God tells Abraham, "I will make of thee a great nation. . . . And I will bless them that bless thee, and curse him that curseth thee." God is concerned about how the world treats His people. The judgment of the

47

"sheep and goats" will be based on how the nations have treated God's people (Matt. 25:31-46). The attitude the disciples were to have toward people as they traveled was determined by the kind of reception they received from them (Luke 9:4-5). When pagan people show kindness toward God's own, He blesses them.

b) In Malta

Acts 28:2 says that the people of Malta "showed . . . no little kindness." That means it wasn't just ordinary politeness, but that they showed extraordinary kindness toward the shipwreck victims. An important topic in conservative, fundamental theology is the depravity of man—that men and women without Jesus Christ are totally sinful and depraved. Yet originally we were made in the image of God, so we find there is something in human nature that sometimes compels people to do kind deeds in times of great need.

2. Pagan kindness illustrated

A classic illustration of such kindness is found in Luke 10:30-37: "Jesus . . . said, A certain man went down from Jerusalem to Jericho, and fell among thieves, who stripped him of his raiment, and wounded him, and departed, leaving him half dead. And by chance there came down a certain priest that way; and when he saw him, he passed by on the other side. And likewise a Levite, when he was at the place, came and looked on him, and passed by on the other side. But a certain Samaritan, as he journeyed, came where he was; and when he saw him, he had compassion on him, and went to him, and bound up his wounds, pouring in oil and wine, and set him on his own beast, and brought him to an inn, and took care of him. And on the next day, when he departed, he took out two denarii, and gave them to the host, and said unto him, Take care of him; and whatever thou spendest more, when I come again, I will repay thee. Which, now, of these three, thinkest thou, was neighbor unto him that fell among the thieves? And he said, He that showed mercy on him. Then said Jesus unto him, Go, and do thou likewise." Here our Lord told about a man who extended kindness to someone in need, although he may not have been a religious man. Even unbelieving people have the capacity to do good things. Some of the greatest philanthropists in the world have been unbelievers.

3. Pagan kindness explained

Romans 2:14-15 says, "When the Gentiles, who have not the law, do by nature the things contained in the law, these, having not the law, are a law unto themselves; who show the work of the law written in their hearts." The kindness of the Maltese people illustrates the internal revelation of God to the pagan. Here we see people without a knowledge of Jesus Christ or the Mosaic law having the sense to do what is right in a time of need. Why? Because the law of God was written in their hearts, their "conscience . . . bearing witness" (v. 16). Verse 27 says, "Shall not uncircumcision [pagans] . . . if [they] fulfill the law, judge thee, who by the letter and circumcision dost transgress the law?" The pagan who obeys the law he knows internally is better off than he who knows the truth but disobeys it.

God has generally revealed Himself to everyone in one way or another—even to pagans. Many people wonder how the heathen can know about God. They can know Him because He has written His law on their hearts —they have a sense of morality, of right and wrong, of kindness and love. So when they eventually hear the specific revelation of His Word, they can know it is true.

II. POTENTIAL HARM (vv. 3-6)

A. Paul's Humble Example (v. 3a)

"When Paul had gathered a bundle of sticks."

1. The example of Paul

Paul was busy gathering brushwood to keep the fire going. He was as anxious to perform the little tasks, such

49

as gathering sticks for a fire, as he was to perform the large tasks, such as confronting Caesar. Since he was a prisoner he may have been chained while he gathered sticks. But in the eyes of the men from the ship, he was not perceived as a prisoner. He had established a great deal of credibility with them—from taking charge when they needed a cool head to forecasting that they would all be spared despite losing the ship (Acts 27:21-44). Yet when it came time to gather sticks, we don't see Paul directing others to do the job; he did it himself.

Many leaders avoid simple, humble, menial tasks because they expect everyone else to do them. But a true spiritual leader will stoop to that level when the occasion calls for it. After fourteen days of fighting a storm, growing weak from lack of food, and enduring an icy swim to shore, you would expect Paul to stay by the fire to keep warm. But it was he who gathered fuel to maintain the fire, while others stayed warm. A true leader has a servant's mentality, and Paul never lost that perspective. He was always making sacrifices for others.

2. The example of Christ

Jesus said, "The Son of man came, not to be ministered unto but to minister, and to give his life a ransom for many" (Mark 10:45). True spiritual leadership includes an eagerness to do the humble task as well as the exalted one. Humility is a must for the servant of God. After washing the disciples' feet Jesus said, "I have given you an example, that ye should do as I have done to you" (John 13:15). Lead with a servant's mentality; stoop to meet the needs of one another. If anyone thinks himself too important to get dirty, wash feet, or pick up sticks, he isn't as important as he thinks.

B. The Snake's Sudden Appearance (vv. 3b-4)

1. Paul's predicament (v. 3b)

"When Paul had gathered a bundle of sticks, and laid them on the fire, there came a viper out of the heat, and fastened on his hand."

A viper is a kind of poisonous snake. Today no such snakes remain on Malta. But at that time they must have been plentiful because the natives immediately recognized the snake and the severity of its bite. The snake was poisonous and was beginning to inject its venom into Paul's hand.

2. The natives' assessment (v. 4)

"When the barbarians saw the venomous beast hang on his hand, they said among themselves, No doubt this man is a murderer, whom, though he hath escaped the sea, yet justice alloweth not to live."

The Greek word translated "justice" (*dikē*) should be capitalized. Albert Barnes wrote that "*Dikē*, or justice, was represented by the heathen as a goddess, the daughter of Jupiter, whose office it was to take vengeance, or inflict punishment for crimes" (*Notes on the New Testament: Acts* [Grand Rapids: Baker, 1975], p. 370). The natives expected Paul to fall dead as one of her victims.

Again we have an illustration of the pagans' innate sense of right and wrong. They understood the concept of justice—sin must be punished. If Paul were to die in this way, they would conclude that he had done something wrong. Romans 1:18-19 shows where this sense of morality comes from: "The wrath of God is revealed from heaven against all ungodliness and unrighteousness of men, who hold the truth in unrighteousness, because that which may be known of God is manifest in them; for God hath shown it unto them." Within man's heart is a sense of love and kindness. Here we see also a sense of morality and justice. However, this sense of morality is inconsistent: pagan religions speak of gods who won't tolerate murder but don't mind adultery and other sins. They make gods to accommodate their desires, but at least a germ of morality is present.

The citizens of Malta manifested kindness and love toward needy strangers—and an understanding that wrong behavior deserves judgment. Notice the contrast between the two: one is a sense of goodness and its consequences; the other is a sense of evil and its consequences. Good and evil are the two sides of morality. It all began when Adam and Eve bit into the forbidden fruit and received the knowledge of good and evil (Gen. 3:6-7). All men and women have that sensitivity within them, and that's why God holds them responsible for their actions. It is likely that as they are faithful to what revelation they have, God will continue to reveal more of His truth to them (e.g., Cornelius in Acts 10).

C. God's Miraculous Deliverance (vv. 5-6)

1. A confirmation from God (v. 5)

"He shook off the beast into the fire, and felt no harm."

That kind of calmness is conspicuous. After receiving a snakebite, most people would run around in a panic, but Paul merely flicked the snake off his hand. God used miracles to confirm the works and deeds of His apostles. That is why this incident took place in the sight of the natives.

2. A change of opinion (v. 6)

"However, they looked when he should have swollen, or fallen down dead suddenly; but after they had looked a great while, and saw no harm come to him, they changed their minds, and said that he was a god."

Pagan theology is subjective. Paul went from being a murderer to being a god in their eyes. However, Paul didn't want that kind of response—he wanted to be perceived as a representative of God.

Paul experienced a similar response earlier in his ministry. Acts 14:8-15 says, "There sat a certain man at Lystra, impotent in his feet, being a cripple from birth, who never had walked. The same heard Paul speak; who, steadfastly beholding him, and perceiving that he had faith to be healed, said with a loud voice, Stand upright on thy feet. And he leaped and walked. And when the people saw what Paul had done, they lifted up their voices, saying in the speech of Lycaonia, The gods are come down to us in the likeness of men. And they called Barnabas, Jupiter; and Paul, Mercurius, because he was the chief speaker. Then the priest of Jupiter, whose temple was before their city, brought oxen and garlands unto the gates, and would have done sacrifice with the people; which when the apostles, Barnabas and Paul, heard of, they tore their clothes, and ran in among the people, crying out, and saying, Sirs, why do ye these things? We also are men of like passions with you, and preach unto you that ye should turn from these vanities unto the living God." Paul and Barnabas wanted no part of their proliferation of deities. They were representatives of the true God.

So it wasn't surprising to Paul that the Maltese people perceived him as a god. But it was important for them to recognize that God's spiritual power prevented his being harmed by the snake. That power enabled Paul to establish the credibility of the gospel.

The people of Malta were idolaters. Perverting the internal revelation God had given them, they had created gods after the image of man, four-footed animals, and creeping things (Rom. 1:23). So when Paul was not harmed by the snake, they perceived him to be a god. Although Paul didn't want that response, it did put him in a position of high esteem and gave him opportunity to minister.

III. PUBLIC HEALING (vv. 7-11)

A. The Setting (v. 7)

1. Publius's title (v. 7a)

"In the same quarters [the vicinity of the shipwreck] were possessions [the estate] of the chief man of the island."

Publius was the number-one citizen of Malta—the man in charge. He lived on a large estate in the vicinity of the shipwreck. F. F. Bruce notes that the title translated "the chief man of the island" appears on two Maltese

53

inscriptions that have been discovered in archaeological digs. One is in Greek and one in Latin. From those inscriptions we know that the leader of the island was called "the chief man" or "the first man" (*Commentary on the Book of Acts* [Grand Rapids: Eerdmans, 1975], p. 523).

2. Publius's estate (v. 7*b*)

"[His] name was Publius, who received us, and lodged us three days courteously."

That gives us an idea of the size of his estate. He put up 276 people for three days. It was only a temporary place for the shipwreck victims—they would have to spend the winter on Malta. But Publius housed them until they could make arrangements for winter quarters.

B. The Problem (v. 8*a*)

"It came to pass that the father of Publius lay sick of a fever and of a bloody flux."

The Greek word translated "fever" (*puretois*) means "gastric fever." It is rendered in the plural, which indicates that it was a recurring gastric upset. The Greek word translated "bloody flux" is *dusenteriō*, from which we derive the English word dysentery, an intestinal disease. F. F. Bruce says, "Malta has long had a peculiarly unpleasant fever of its own—'Malta Fever,' due to a microbe in goats' milk" (p. 523).

C. The Solution (v. 8*b*)

"To whom Paul entered in, and prayed, and laid his hands on him, and healed him."

1. Paul's healing ministry

Paul did two things: he prayed and laid his hands on him. Why did he pray? Because all power is from God. Why did he lay his hands on him? Because he wanted Publius and his father to see it was God's power that brought about healing and that Paul was the agent of that power.

2. Paul's preaching ministry

I am convinced that Paul also preached to them. I think the reason his preaching is not mentioned in the text is that it is obvious. Christ didn't perform miracles without pointing out that they corroborated the testimony of the gospel. When Peter performed miracles he preached Christ (e.g., Acts 3:1–4:4). The same was true of Paul (e.g., Acts 19:11-19). So when Paul healed, we can be sure he preached. According to tradition, Paul founded a church at Malta, and Publius became the first pastor.

D. The Reaction (vv. 9-10)

1. What the people received (v. 9)

"When this was done, others also in the island, who had diseases, came and were healed."

God showed kindness to those who had been kind to His representatives (Paul and Luke). He also established Paul's credibility. Since Paul remained on the island three months until winter passed, he had plenty of opportunity to follow up that confirmation with the gospel.

2. What the people gave (v. 10)

"Who also honored us with many honors, and when we departed, they placed on board such things as were necessary."

Three months of preaching the gospel would result in one of two things: making Christians or making enemies. It is hard to imagine that the people would bestow honors on Paul if they were upset with him for dealing truthfully with their pagan religion. This indicates that many of them became believers and that a church may already have been founded on Malta.

E. The Departure (v. 11)

"After three months we departed in a ship of Alexandria, which had wintered in the isle, whose sign was Castor and Pollux."

After spending three months of winter there, it was now time to leave. Paul, Luke, the other prisoners, the soldiers, and the crew boarded another ship that was probably similar to the one that had brought them to Malta. Castor and Pollux are names of the twins in the Gemini constellation. They were the mythical sons of Jupiter and considered to be the patrons of navigation. Navigators and sailors looked to them for security and safety, so their images were carved on this particular ship.

IV. PAUL'S HOPE (vv. 12-15)

A. The Journey to Puteoli (vv. 12-14a)

1. The itinerary (vv. 12-13)

"Landing at Syracuse, we tarried there three days. And from there we fetched a compass [they tacked], and came to Rhegium; and after one day the south wind blew, and we came the next day to Puteoli."

Puteoli is a port in the bay of Naples. Today it's called Pozzuoli. In the past it was a chief port for the grain fleet. Since Puteoli was about 145 miles southwest of Rome, the grain would still have to be transported by land after arriving in port.

2. The reception (v. 14a)

"Where we found brethren, and were desired to tarry with them seven days."

There was a large Jewish community in Puteoli. Since the city was a trade center like Corinth, Ephesus, or Antioch, many Jewish traders were there. Some commentators think that the churches at Puteoli and at Rome could have been founded as early as A.D. 50-60, so it's possible that Luke was referring to fellow Christians when he said, "We found brethren."

B. The Journey to Rome (vv. 14b-15)

1. The reception (vv. 14b-15a)

"So we went toward Rome. And from there, when the brethren heard of us, they came to meet us as far as the Forum of Appius, and The Three Taverns."

Paul would have had to travel from Puteoli to Rome on the Appian Way, named for Appius Claudius Caecus, the commissioning builder. All the way Paul was concerned about the kind of response he would receive from the Roman believers.

2. The result (v. 15b)

"Whom when Paul saw, he thanked God, and took courage."

As he arrived in the caravan, chained as a prisoner, Paul was greeted by the brethren. And that encouraged him. He was thrilled with this reception. It had been about three years since he wrote the epistle to the Romans and told them how he desired to come and minister to them (Rom. 15:24, 32).

V. PRIVATE HOUSING (v. 16)

"When we came to Rome, the centurion delivered the prisoners to the captain of the guard; but Paul was permitted to dwell by himself with a soldier that kept him."

Paul was imprisoned in a house, chained to a Roman soldier (v. 20). I imagine whoever Paul was chained to heard the gospel often!

Conclusion

In this passage we have witnessed God's faithfulness to a faithful man.

A. God Surrounds His Servant with Kindness

Acts 27:2-3 tells us that Paul arrived in Sidon from Caesarea and immediately was refreshed and ministered to by the believers there. In Acts 28:1-2 we see his needs were met by the Maltese people. In verse 10 we read that they honored him.

B. God Ministers to His Servant's Needs

The believers in Sidon ministered to Paul's medical needs (27:3). Publius provided Paul with lodging (28:7). The Maltese people gave him what he needed (v. 10). The brethren in Puteoli ministered to him (v. 14).

C. God Encourages His Servant

When the ship was being battered about by the storm, God sent an angel to Paul to encourage him (27:22-25). Paul in turn encouraged the men on board the ship. But the greatest encouragement may have been the Roman Christians' meeting him some forty-three miles from Rome to express their love and affection (28:15).

D. God Protects His Servant from Harm

God rescued Paul from a terrible storm and a shipwreck (27:14-44). God also saved him from a snakebite (28:4-5).

E. God Blesses His Servant's Influence

Wherever Paul went, dramatic things took place. He had such a dynamic influence on those on board ship that it is probable some of them came to know Jesus Christ. He had such an impact on Malta that a church began there. We know he had a profound impact in Rome because many in Caesar's household were saved (Phil. 4:22).

F. God Fulfills His Servant's Desire

>   Paul wanted to go to Rome, and he succeeded in getting
>   there. He wanted to be encouraged by the Christians there,
>   and he was (28:15).

Paul was a faithful man who exhibited all the necessary qualities of
a faithful leader. In turn God blessed him. Proverbs 28:20 says, "A
faithful man shall abound with blessings." God is faithful, and He
rewards those who faithfully serve Him.

Focusing on the Facts

1. What is one of the great virtues of Christianity (see p. 45)?
2. How did the shipwreck victims conclude that they had landed
   on the island of Malta (see pp. 46-47)?
3. What is a better translation of the Greek word *barbaros* than
   "barbarous"? Why is that significant (see p. 47)?
4. What does God generally do for people who show kindness to
   His people (see pp. 47-48)?
5. Characterize the kindness that the Maltese people showed the
   shipwreck victims (see p. 48).
6. What did the kindness of the Maltese people reveal about them
   (see p. 49)?
7. In what way did Paul exemplify humble leadership while on
   Malta (Acts 28:3; see pp. 49-50)?
8. What did Jesus teach about the necessity for humility in leadership (see p. 50)?
9. What did the Maltese people initially believe about why Paul
   was bitten by the snake (Acts 28:4; see p. 51)?
10. What are the two sides of morality? Explain (see p. 52).
11. What caused the Maltese people to change their minds about
    Paul? How did they later perceive him (see pp. 52-53)?
12. Who was Publius? What did he do for the shipwreck victims
    (see pp. 53-54)?
13. How did the illness of Publius's father give Paul an opportuni-
    ty to preach the gospel (see pp. 54-55)?
14. How did God show kindness to the Maltese people (Acts 28:9;
    see p. 55)?
15. Why can we conclude that many of the Maltese people became
    believers (Acts 28:10; see pp. 55-56)?

16. How did Paul respond when he was met by many believers from Rome (Acts 28:15; see p. 57)?
17. Cite the six ways God blessed Paul (see pp. 58-59).

Pondering the Principles

1. Romans 12:13 commands believers to be hospitable. First Peter 4:9 says we are to be hospitable to one another "without grudging." That indicates it's not always easy. Yet both those verses are in the form of commands. How do you need to improve in your hospitality, both toward believers and unbelievers? Commit yourself to improvement in this area. Ask God to give you opportunities to be hospitable to others. Invite to your home someone you don't know well—you might be surprised by the blessings God will give you through your time of fellowship.

2. Review the six ways God blessed Paul for his faithfulness. Looking back over your Christian life, record some of the ways in which God has surrounded you with kindness, met your needs, encouraged you, protected you from harm, blessed your influence, and fulfilled your desires. What should be your response to all that He has done for you?

4

The Story That Never Ends

Outline

Introduction

Lesson
  I. Paul's Introduction (vv. 17-20)
     A. Paul's Pattern Examined (v. 17a)
        1. Paul's love for the Jews
           a) Romans 9:1-3
           b) Romans 10:1
        2. The Jews' interest in Paul
     B. Paul's Imprisonment Explained (vv. 17b-20)
        1. His innocence (vv. 17b-18)
           a) Portrayed (v. 17b)
           b) Proved (v. 18)
        2. His appeal (v. 19a)
        3. His love (v. 19b)
        4. His reasoning (v. 20)
 II. The Jewish Leaders' Interest (vv. 21-22)
     A. No Report
     B. No Accusation
III. Paul's Invitation (vv. 23-24)
     A. The Content of Paul's Message (v. 23)
     B. The Response to Paul's Message (v. 24)
 IV. The Gospel's Inversion (vv. 25-29)
     A. God's Plan for Israel (vv. 25-27)
        1. Israel's willful rejection
        2. Israel's eventual restoration
           a) Grafting in the Gentiles
           b) Regrafting in Israel
     B. God's Plan for the Gentiles (vv. 28-29)
  V. The Story's Incompletion (vv. 30-31)

Conclusion
A. Where Paul Preached
B. How Paul Preached
   1. Lovingly
   2. Biblically
   3. Doctrinally
C. When Paul Preached
D. To Whom Paul Preached
E. What Paul Preached

Introduction

The last section of Acts concludes the first chapter of early church history. In Acts the Holy Spirit has recorded the first historical account of the early church. At the beginning of this book our Lord Jesus Christ said to the disciples, "Ye shall receive power, after the Holy Spirit is come upon you; and ye shall be witnesses unto me both in Jerusalem, and in all Judaea, and in Samaria, and unto the uttermost part of the earth" (Acts 1:8). That is the theme of the book of Acts. The gospel began in Jerusalem, then spread throughout all Judea, Samaria, and finally to the uttermost part of the earth. By the end of Acts it had spread to Rome.

At this point the record stops, but the story of the church continues throughout eternity. In that sense Acts is an unfinished book. In fact, it ends so abruptly that many have thought a chapter or paragraph was lost: "Paul dwelt two whole years in his own hired house, and received all that came in unto him, preaching the kingdom of God, and teaching those things which concern the Lord Jesus Christ, with all confidence, no man forbidding him" (Acts 28:30-31). It doesn't say what became of Paul at the end of the two years. It doesn't tell us about the growth of the church in Rome. But this incomplete ending is by design of the Holy Spirit because the church has no end. Only the record ceases to be written.

Although the record is incomplete, enough has been written to reveal the source of power for the church—the Holy Spirit. Enough has been written to reveal the pattern of blessing for the church —walking by the Spirit. Enough has been written to indicate what the church's approach to evangelism ought to be—declaring Jesus Christ. Enough has been written to warn of the perils to the church

—sin, discipline, and judgment. Enough has been written to establish the priorities of the church—teaching the Word of God and reaching those who don't know Christ. And enough has been written elsewhere to show what the church is to be by example. Paul laid out the principles of the church in Ephesians, 1 and 2 Timothy, and Titus.

Lesson

In Acts 28:17-31 we will look at the close of the book of Acts, as the church spreads to Rome, where Paul finally arrives after many years of longing. Acts closes with Paul in chains in the midst of a tremendous mission field. His first approach to evangelism in this situation is recorded for us, beginning in verse 17. It's fitting that the book of Acts should end with evangelism. Believers today are continuing the world evangelism that began in Acts. And it is my prayer that we continue that effort.

Let us look first at the historical narrative and then highlight its emphasis on evangelism.

I. PAUL'S INTRODUCTION (vv. 17-20)

First Paul had to introduce himself to the people of Rome. Now that he had arrived, he wanted to have an impact on the total city. It's difficult to have an impact on more than a million people, but Paul had a strategy.

A. Paul's Pattern Examined (v. 17a)

"It came to pass that, after three days, Paul called the chief of the Jews together."

The chief of the Jews would have been more than one person. F. F. Bruce tells us "we have references in Roman inscriptions to at least seven Jewish synagogues in Rome" (*Commentary on the Book of Acts* [Grand Rapids: Eerdmans], pp. 63, 530). Each of those synagogues would have been represented by a chief man. They were most likely represented by Jewish people who had important responsibilities in the city. Some may have been wealthy merchants.

Paul's pattern, as always, was to go to the Jews first whenever he entered a city. That's because he found an initial openness among them. Also, if he went to the Gentiles first, he would have alienated himself from the Jews.

1. Paul's love for the Jews

Although Paul has been accused of anti-Semitism by many Jewish people throughout history, he held no such attitude. Although he had been maligned, persecuted, threatened, beaten, and abused mainly by Jewish religious leaders for several years before arriving in Rome, he felt no animosity toward them or the people. That he went to them first reveals his love for Israel.

a) Romans 9:1-3—Paul said, "I say the truth in Christ, I lie not, my conscience also bearing me witness in the Holy Spirit, that I have great heaviness and continual sorrow in my heart. For I could wish that I myself were accursed from Christ for my brethren, my kinsmen according to the flesh." Paul loved Israel so much that he would wish himself accursed if it would be to their benefit.

b) Romans 10:1—Paul said, "My heart's desire and prayer to God for Israel is, that they might be saved." Paul's love for Israel was undiminished by all he had endured at their hands.

2. The Jews' interest in Paul

Since Paul was a prisoner he couldn't go to the synagogues to speak to the people, so he asked the chief men to come to him, and they did. They would have had a deep interest in him since they certainly had heard something about him. He had become popular in the Roman world just as he had become unpopular in the Jewish world. He had disrupted every synagogue he entered by winning some to Jesus Christ. The reports about his endeavors had certainly reached the Jewish population at Rome. They definitely would have been interested in what he had to say about the Messiah.

Acts 18:2 tells us Emperor Claudius had commanded all the Jews to leave Rome. Apparently, since Nero was now emperor, that edict was no longer in effect.

B. Paul's Imprisonment Explained (vv. 17b-20)

Paul had to explain a delicate matter. He had to prove he was innocent of the charges brought against him by the Jewish leaders in Jerusalem, yet at the same time avoid alienating his Jewish audience.

1. His innocence (vv. 17b-18)

   a) Portrayed (v. 17b)

   "When they were come together, he said unto them, Men and brethren, though I have committed nothing against the people or customs of our fathers, yet was I delivered prisoner from Jerusalem into the hands of the Romans."

   Paul had not violated Jewish law, and he had not injured Jewish people. He had done absolutely nothing wrong; he was innocent of any crime. Although his imprisonment was caused by Jewish antagonism against him, that imprisonment did not reflect any anti-Semitic crime against the customs of the people, the law of God, or God Himself.

   The Jewish leaders in Jerusalem had accused Paul of sedition, claiming he was a reactionary against the Roman government. They also accused him of sectarianism, claiming he was a leader in the sect of the Nazarenes and thus a heretic. And they accused him of sacrilege, saying he had profaned the Temple and therefore had blasphemed God. Acts 24:5-6 records those accusations: "We have found this man a pestilent fellow, and a mover of sedition among all the Jews throughout the world, and a ringleader of the sect of the Nazarenes, who also hath gone about to profane the temple."

b) Proved (v. 18)

"Who, when they [the Romans] had examined me, would have let me go, because there was no cause of death in me."

Paul established at the outset that he was innocent in the eyes of the Roman government. In other words he was saying that the Jewish leaders were responsible for his imprisonment. Paul had been taken before the Roman governor Felix and was found innocent (Acts 24). He was taken before Festus, the next Roman governor, and found innocent (Acts 25:1-12). He was then brought by Festus before King Agrippa and again found to be innocent (Acts 25:13–26:32). Even a hearing before the Sanhedrin in Jerusalem proved his innocence, because the Pharisees and Sadducees were divided over his guilt or innocence (Acts 22:30–23:10).

Despite his innocence, Paul was a prisoner. He didn't become one as a result of guilt but because the Romans were being blackmailed by the Jewish leaders. If the Romans didn't punish him, the leaders were likely to mount an insurrection against Rome. That was something Festus wished to avoid (Acts 24:27), so he succumbed to the pressure of the Jewish leaders and kept Paul a prisoner.

2. His appeal (v. 19*a*)

"But when the Jews spoke against it, I was constrained to appeal unto Caesar."

Although Paul was innocent, the Jewish leaders kept up the pressure to the point that his only escape was to appeal to Caesar in the hope of receiving a fair trial. Since he was a Roman citizen, he had the right to appeal his case to Rome. That led to his being transported there.

3. His love (v. 19*b*)

"Not that I had anything to accuse my nation of."

Since he had revealed that the Jewish leaders were responsible for his imprisonment, Paul was quick to point out that he was just defending himself against unfair accusations and that in no way was he condemning or attacking the Jewish people or nation. He was not a traitor to the cause of Judaism. He remained Jewish in nationality and interest. He maintained his special love for the people. He held no bitterness toward Israel. He was simply defending himself.

4. His reasoning (v. 20)

"For this cause, therefore, have I called for you, to see you, and to speak with you, because for the hope of Israel I am bound with this chain."

Here Paul gave the reason for the antagonism against him: the hope of Israel. Who is the hope of Israel? The Messiah. Paul's trouble was the result of preaching that Jesus was the Messiah, that He rose from the dead, and that He provides resurrection for all who believe in Him. That was the real issue. For that reason he was in chains.

The Hope of Israel

1. Paul's testimony before the Sanhedrin

Acts 23:6 says, "When Paul perceived that the one part were Sadducees, and the other Pharisees, he cried out in the council, Men and brethren, I am a Pharisee, the son of a Pharisee; of the hope and resurrection of the dead I am called in question." The hope of Israel relates to the Messiah and the resurrection. The Jewish people knew that God had promised a coming Messiah and that He would usher in a glorious kingdom. For those who had already died to share in that kingdom, there would have to be a resurrection.

a) Isaiah 26:19—The prophet Isaiah said, "Thy dead men shall live, together with my dead body shall they arise. Awake and sing, ye that dwell in dust; for thy dew is like the dew of the herbs, and the earth shall cast out the dead."

b) Job 19:26—Job said, "Though after my skin worms destroy this body, yet in my flesh shall I see God."

c) Daniel 12:2—"Many of those who sleep in the dust of the earth shall awake, some to everlasting life, and some to shame and everlasting contempt."

2. Paul's testimony before Felix

In Acts 24:15 Paul says, "[I] have hope toward God, which they themselves [the Jewish leaders] also allow, that there shall be a resurrection of the dead."

3. Paul's testimony before Agrippa

In Acts 26:6-8 he says, "Now I stand and am judged for the hope of the promise made of God unto our fathers, unto which promise our twelve tribes, earnestly serving God day and night, hope to come. For which hope's sake, King Agrippa, I am accused by the Jews. Why should it be thought a thing incredible with you, that God should raise the dead?"

The hope of Israel is that there will be a resurrection of the dead.

Paul said that he was in chains because he had been declaring that the Messiah had arrived and had risen from the dead, thus providing for the resurrection of the dead. I imagine that as he said, "I am bound with this chain" (Acts 28:20), he probably held up the chain so that they could see it. Paul constantly referred to his chains. In Ephesians 6:20 he says, "I am an ambassador in bonds." In 2 Timothy 1:16 he says, "The Lord give mercy unto the house of Onesiphorus, for he often refreshed me, and was not ashamed of my chain."

II. THE JEWISH LEADERS' INTEREST (vv. 21-22)

"They said unto him, We neither received letters out of Judaea concerning thee, neither any of the brethren that came showed or spoke any harm of thee. But we desire to hear of thee what thou thinkest; for as concerning this sect [Christianity], we know that everywhere it is spoken against."

The Jewish leaders in Rome displayed a very diplomatic attitude. They denied any knowledge of Paul's case, and they were eager to hear what he had to say about Christianity, about which they had heard only negative things.

A. No Report

Amazingly enough, they had received no word from Judea about Paul. The ship Paul arrived on may have been the most recent ship to come from Judea to Rome. It had left later than scheduled and at a time that was becoming dangerous for ships to sail the Mediterranean (Acts 27:9). When the Roman government in Judea had determined to send Paul to Rome, it was only a matter of days before he was on a ship. So it is likely that Paul was on the first ship that had sailed from Judea to Rome since his trial before Agrippa.

B. No Accusation

Another reason that the Jewish leaders in Rome had no report about Paul is that apparently the Sanhedrin was reluctant to pursue its case to Rome. They knew they didn't have a case. So far they had been unsuccessful in presenting it before the provincial rulers, and they may have been fearful of looking bad to Caesar. The Roman government looked harshly upon anyone who prosecuted a case without strong evidence. It would have been difficult to prosecute Paul, a Roman citizen, in Rome when they didn't have a case. There also would have been favorable information about Paul from Festus and Felix. So it is possible they were satisfied in having Paul removed from Judea and therefore saw no need to send anyone to inform the Roman Jews.

III. PAUL'S INVITATION (vv. 23-24)

Having seen their openness and interest, Paul established a time to make his presentation. All the Jewish leaders gathered to hear him speak.

A. The Content of Paul's Message (v. 23)

"When they had appointed him a day, there came many to him into his lodging, to whom he expounded and testified the kingdom of God, persuading them concerning Jesus, both out of the law of Moses, and out of the prophets, from morning to evening."

The general meaning of the phrase "the kingdom of God" is the rule of God in the universe. Paul focused on persuading the leaders that Jesus is the king of the kingdom—the Messiah. And he used the Old Testament Law and Prophets as his proof.

Paul used the same approach throughout the book of Acts. He labored to prove the gospel of Jesus Christ as the true and necessary fulfillment of Israel's Scripture—of Old Testament history, typology, and prophecy. I'm convinced Paul didn't preach a sermon but engaged in a dialogue with the Jewish leaders.

B. The Response to Paul's Message (v. 24)

"Some believed the things that were spoken, and some believed not."

That is the typical response to the preaching of the gospel. Some believe, and some don't. Both Greek verbs are in the imperfect tense, implying continuous, progressive action. The simplicity of salvation is that it is reduced to this: a person either believes in Christ or he doesn't.

It is significant that some didn't believe. The gospel had been continually offered to Israel. However rejection was the primary response. Christ never received national acceptance—only a small remnant believed.

IV. THE GOSPEL'S INVERSION (vv. 25-29)

An inversion is a reversal. The gospel went to the Jew first (Rom. 1:16), but we see that priority reversed in the following verses. For the fourth time in Scripture the Spirit of God quotes a prophecy first recorded in Isaiah 6:9-10. Isaiah spoke those words at a time when Israel was in sin. Our Lord Jesus quotes him in Matthew 13:14-15 to pronounce judgment on Israel. John quotes the same passage in John 12:40. Finally Paul quotes it in Acts 28:25-27.

A. God's Plan for Israel (vv. 25-27)

"When they agreed not among themselves, they departed, after Paul had spoken one word, Well spoke the Holy Spirit by Isaiah, the prophet, unto our fathers, saying, Go unto this people, and say, Hearing ye shall hear, and shall not understand; and seeing ye shall see, and not perceive; for the heart of this people is become obtuse, and their ears are dull of hearing, and their eyes have they closed; lest they should see with their eyes, and hear with their ears, and understand with their heart, and should be converted, and I should heal them."

What began as a willful act on the part of Israel became God's sovereign plan. Israel rejected God, becoming blind and deaf in their spiritual understanding. Consequently they decided their own destiny, as God sealed their ears, eyes, and minds.

1. Israel's willful rejection

Jesus came into the world born of a virgin. As God incarnate He lived in humility among men and women in Nazareth for thirty relatively obscure years. Then He announced to Israel that He was God, the Messiah, the living Christ, the living water, the bread of life, the light of the world, the good shepherd, the resurrection and the life—all titles attributed to Him in John's gospel. He substantiated all those claims by miracles, signs, matchless words, and unsurpassed love.

What was the response of Israel? They doubted Him, denied Him, rejected Him, and ultimately executed Him. We see Jesus' final call to Israel in John 12:35-40: "Jesus said unto them, Yet a little while is the light with you. Walk while ye have the light, lest darkness come upon you; for he that walketh in darkness knoweth not where he goeth. While ye have light, believe in the light, that ye may be the sons of light. These things spoke Jesus, and departed, and did hide himself from

71

them. But though he had done so many miracles before them, yet they believed not on him; that the saying of Isaiah, the prophet, might be fulfilled, which he spoke, Lord, who hath believed our report? And to whom hath the arm of the Lord been revealed? Therefore, they could not believe, because that Isaiah said again, He hath blinded their eyes, and hardened their heart; that they should not see with their eyes, nor understand with their heart, and be converted, and I should heal them." What began as willful blindness turned into sovereign blindness. He who will not believe may find one day that he cannot believe.

2. Israel's eventual restoration

Nevertheless God is not through with Israel. He did abandon Israel when they abandoned Christ, but not permanently. Israel's unbelief caused God to set the nation aside temporarily. Romans 9:17-18 says, "The scripture saith unto Pharaoh, Even for this same purpose have I raised thee up, that I might show my power in thee, and that my name might be declared throughout all the earth. Therefore hath he mercy on whom he will have mercy, and whom he will he hardeneth." This is God's sovereign choice: He will save whom He will save, and He will gain glory from whom He will gain glory.

a) Grafting in the Gentiles

For now God has chosen to go to the Gentiles: "I will call them my people, who were not my people; and her beloved, who was not beloved" (Rom. 9:25). Here God indicates that the Gentiles would take Israel's place. Then Paul said, "The Gentiles, who followed not after righteousness, have attained to righteousness, even the righteousness which is of faith; but Israel, who followed after the law of righteousness, hath not attained to the law of righteousness" (vv. 30-31).

In Romans 11 the natural branches represent Israel, the wild olive branches represent the Gentiles, and the trunk is the blessing of God. Paul says, "If some of the branches be broken off, and thou, being a wild olive tree, were grafted in among them . . . boast not against the branches. But if thou boast, thou bearest not the root, but the root thee. Thou wilt say, then, The branches were broken off, that I might be grafted in. Well, because of unbelief they were broken off, and thou standest by faith. Be not high-minded, but fear; for if God spared not the natural branches, take heed lest he also spare not thee. Behold, therefore, the goodness and severity of God: on them who fell, severity; but toward thee, goodness, if thou continue in his goodness; otherwise thou also shalt be cut off" (vv. 17-22).

b) Regrafting in Israel

In Romans 11:23 Paul says, "They also, if they abide not still in unbelief, shall be grafted in." Israel will be regrafted in if they believe. Paul continues, "For God is able to graft them in again. For if thou wert cut out of the olive tree which is wild by nature, and wert grafted contrary to nature into a good olive tree, how much more shall these, who are the natural branches, be grafted into their own olive tree. . . . Blindness in part is happened to Israel, until the fullness of the Gentiles be come in" (vv. 23-25). All Israel will be saved (v. 26); God will graft them in again. God is not ultimately through with Israel, because He will not break His eternal covenant with them. But for the time being, God has set Israel aside and is giving Gentiles the opportunity to come to Him.

B. God's Plan for the Gentiles (vv. 28-29)

"Be it known, therefore, unto you, that the salvation of God is sent unto the Gentiles, and that they will hear it. And when he had said these words, the Jews departed and had great disputing among themselves."

The book of Acts chronicles how God's Word went to the Gentiles (9:15; 11:18; 13:46-47; 14:27; 15:14-18; 18:6). Nevertheless He will one day restore Israel.

73

V. THE STORY'S INCOMPLETION (vv. 30-31)

"Paul dwelt two whole years in his own hired house, and received all that came in unto him, preaching the kingdom of God, and teaching those things which concern the Lord Jesus Christ, with all confidence, no man forbidding him."

For two years Paul proclaimed Christ under the complacent eye of the Roman authority. He preached about the kingdom of God and about the Lord Jesus Christ, the promised Messiah. What Paul did after that time is left unrecorded in Scripture.

Why Was Paul a Prisoner for Two Years?

Since Paul was innocent, why did he have to remain under house arrest for two years? It's possible that the records about him sent from the Roman governor in Judea were lost in the shipwreck. Sending back to Judea to get copies and having them returned would have taken some time. In addition, Roman law required the accusers or those prosecuting the case to be present in Rome to accuse the prisoner. I have serious doubts that any of the Jewish leaders came to Rome to prosecute him. It is likely that there was an eighteen- or twenty-four-month statutory period in which a case had to be prosecuted. If at the end of that time the prosecution failed to state its case, the prisoner would be released. It is my conviction that at the end of those two years Paul was released. From church tradition we learn that Paul then ministered for some time before he was imprisoned a second time in Rome, and then beheaded.

For two years Paul was able to minister in Rome while a prisoner. In those two years he led many people to Christ. He wrote epistles to the Colossians, to Philemon, to the Ephesians and the Philippians. Many who served him could come and go. He told the Colossians that Aristarchus, Luke, Mark, Jesus Justus, Epaphras, and Demas were with him (4:10-14). He told the Philippians about his blessings and how the gospel was spreading—his bonds being manifest throughout the palace (1:12-14). In Philippians 4:22 he says, "All the saints greet you, chiefly they that are of Caesar's household."

Conclusion

What does Acts 28:17-31 teach us about Paul's method of evangelism?

A. Where Paul Preached

Paul preached the gospel anywhere. He was a prisoner in chains (vv. 16, 20). He was restricted to his own hired house (vv. 23, 30). Yet he was always preaching (v. 31). Paul knew no restriction to his pulpit. If he was in a prison, he preached there. If he was in a marketplace, he preached there. If he was in a synagogue, he preached there. It didn't matter where he was. Evangelism can occur anywhere.

B. How Paul Preached

1. Lovingly

Acts 28:17-20 shows he was sensitive and conciliatory to the Roman Jewish leaders. He told them he didn't have any accusation against the nation of Israel.

2. Biblically

Paul expounded and testified about the kingdom of God as recorded in the Law of Moses and the Prophets (v. 23). He wasn't giving his opinion; he showed how biblical truth about the Messiah was fulfilled in the Lord Jesus Christ.

3. Doctrinally

He taught the great doctrines about the kingdom and the Lord Jesus (vv. 23, 31).

C. When Paul Preached

Paul preached promptly (v. 17)—he gathered an audience after he had been in Rome only three days. He preached tirelessly (v. 23)—from morning to evening. He preached incessantly (vv. 30-31)—for two whole years. He preached boldly (v. 31)—with all confidence.

D. To Whom Paul Preached

Paul preached to both Jews (v. 17) and Gentiles (v. 28). He was willing to speak to anyone.

E. What Paul Preached

Paul attempted to persuade people about Christ (v. 23). He wanted them to know everything about Him (v. 31).

Where are we to preach? Wherever we are. How are we to preach? Lovingly, biblically, and doctrinally. When are we to preach? Promptly, tirelessly, incessantly, and boldly. To whom are we to preach? Jew or Gentile—to anyone. What are we to preach? Jesus Christ. What will the results be? Verse 24 tells us that some will believe and some won't. May we follow Paul's example and preach the truth to whoever will listen, leaving the results to God.

Focusing on the Facts

1. In what ways has enough been written in Acts to benefit the church (see pp. 62-63)?
2. With whom did Paul first ask to meet after he arrived in Rome (Acts 28:17; see p. 63)?
3. Why did Paul go to the Jews first whenever he entered a city for the first time (see p. 64)?
4. What didn't Paul's imprisonment reflect concerning the Jewish people (Acts 28:17; see p. 65)?
5. Of what did the Jewish leaders from Jerusalem accuse Paul (Acts 24:5-6; see p. 65)?
6. What did the Roman leaders in Judea conclude about Paul (Acts 28:18; see p. 66)?
7. Why did Paul remain a prisoner and get sent to Rome (Acts 28:19; see p. 66)?
8. What was the real issue that antagonized the Jewish leadership in Jerusalem (Acts 28:20; see p. 67)?
9. What is the hope of Israel (see pp. 67-68)?

10. Why might the Jewish leaders in Rome not have received a report about Paul (see p. 69)?

11. Why might the Jewish leaders in Jerusalem have decided not to pursue Paul's case to Rome (see p. 69)?

12. What was the content of Paul's message to the Roman Jewish leaders (Acts 28:23; see p. 70)?

13. How did those leaders respond (Acts 28:24; see p. 70)?

14. What was the conclusion to Israel's willful rejection of God (Acts 28:25-27; see pp. 71-72)?

15. Using the imagery of an olive tree, how did God include the Gentiles in His plan (Rom. 11:17-22; see pp. 72-73)?

16. Using the same imagery, what will become of Israel (Rom. 11:23-26; see p. 73)?

17. Why did Paul remain a prisoner in Rome for two years (see p. 74)?

18. What did Paul do during those two years (Acts 28:30-31; see p. 74)?

19. What does Acts 28:17-31 illustrate about Paul's method of evangelism (see pp. 75-76)?

Pondering the Principles

1. Review the introductory section that discusses what Acts teaches about the church (pp. 62-63). Implement the following study for the next couple of weeks. Read through the book of Acts. Record each incident of the Holy Spirit's being the source of power for the church, of walking in the Spirit as the pattern of blessing for the church, and of declaring Jesus Christ as the church's approach to evangelism. Record every incident of warning to the church, and note what form that warning takes. Record every occasion where the priority of the church is clearly delineated. What are you doing within your church to help the worldwide church be what God wants it to be? What do you need to do? Begin today to fulfill your role within God's eternal program.

2. Review Paul's method of evangelism (see pp. 75-76). Where can you proclaim Christ? Make a list of all the different places you will be during the next month. How should you proclaim the gospel? If you feel less than adequate in this area, sign up for some evangelism seminars at your church or one nearby, or go

witnessing with a mature Christian friend. When should you proclaim Christ? Keep in mind that it never mattered to Paul what his circumstances were. To whom should you talk about Christ? Make a list of people whom you know aren't saved. If you haven't already done so, begin to talk to them of your faith in Christ and the wonders of salvation in Him.

Scripture Index

Topical Index

Paul
blessings of, 44, 58-60
evangelism of. *See* preaching of
example of, 40, 42, 49-50
friends of, 10-13, 25, 57
healing ministry of, 54-55
his love for Israel, 64, 66-67
house arrest of. *See* imprisonment of
humility of, 49-50
illness of, 12-13, 37, 58
imprisonment of, 57, 62-76
influence of, 22-24, 58
innocence of, 65-66, 74
leadership of, 9, 28, 36-41
personality of, 9
preaching of, 55, 70, 75-78
shipwreck experienced by, 8-24, 28-41, 45
snakebite experienced by, 50-53
Preaching
content of, 55, 70
method of, 70, 75-78.

See also Leadership
Providence of God. *See* God
Publius
estate of, 54
his father's illness, 54-55
title of, 53-54

Responsibility, and God's sovereignty, 32-33, 40-41
Resurrection
the hope of, 67-68
Old Testament teaching on, 67-68

Service
key to, 32
leadership. *See* Leadership
Shipwreck, Paul's. *See* Paul
Sidon, the church at, 12-13
Society, preservation of, 23-24
Sovereignty of God. *See* God

Trustworthiness of God. *See* God, faithfulness of